D1304162

Journey to Freedom

MUHAMMAD ALI

BY CLAY LATIMER

"IT IS THE HEART THAT MAKES
ONE GREAT OR SMALL."

～ MUHAMMAD ALI ～

Cover and page 4 caption:
Cassius Clay trains at City
Parks Gym in New York in
February of 1962.

Content Consultant:
Susan Shaffer Nahmias,
Chief Curator, Muhammad
Ali Center

Published in the United States of America by The Child's World®
1980 Lookout Drive, Mankato, MN 56003-1705
800-599-READ • www.childsworld.com

ACKNOWLEDGEMENTS

The Child's World®: Mary Berendes, Publishing Director

The Design Lab: Kathleen Petelinsek, Design; Gregory Lindholm, Page Production

Red Line Editorial: Amy Van Zee, Editorial Direction

PHOTOS

Cover and page 4: AP Images

Interior: AP Images, 5, 9, 10, 11, 13, 15, 17, 18, 19, 20, 23, 24; Bettmann/Corbis, 6, 14; Doug Mills/AP Images, 25; Ed Reinke/AP Images, 27; ES/AP Images, 8; Mark D. Phillips/AP Images, 26; Shawano Cleary/AP Images, 7; Tony Camerano/AP Images, 21

LIBRARY OF CONGRESS CATALOGING-IN-PUBLICATION DATA

Latimer, Clay, 1952–

 Muhammad Ali / by Clay Latimer.

    p. cm. — (Journey to freedom)

 Includes bibliographical references and index.

 ISBN 978-1-60253-132-1 (library bound : alk. paper)

 1. Ali, Muhammad, 1942——Juvenile literature. 2. Boxers (Sports)—United States—Biography—Juvenile literature. I. Title.

 GV1132.A4L38 2009

 796.83092—dc22

 [B]

                              2008031936

CONTENTS

Chapter One

THE START OF SOMETHING BIG

welve-year-old Cassius Clay couldn't believe his bad luck. He had ridden his new bicycle to the Columbia Auditorium in his hometown of Louisville, Kentucky. He parked it carefully outside. Inside the auditorium was the annual Louisville Home Show. Cassius and a friend wandered from booth to booth for hours. They stuffed themselves with popcorn and candy. They joked around and enjoyed themselves. Finally, it was time to go home.

The boys went back to find their bicycles. But Cassius's shiny, red bike was gone! He looked all around. It was nowhere to be seen. Cassius was stunned. Someone told Cassius that in the basement of the building was a policeman who could help him find his bike. He returned to the building in search of Joe Martin, a white policeman.

Cassius was furious. He told Joe Martin that he would "whup" whoever had taken his bike. Joe Martin told the angry boy that if he was going to challenge the person who had taken his bike, he had better learn how to fight. Cassius looked around the basement and realized he was in a gym. He saw something that would change his life forever: a boxing ring.

Cassius Clay trained hard to become a successful athlete. He practices here in 1963.

Cassius forgot all about his bike. He asked the men at the gym if he could come back sometime to learn how to box. Cassius returned again very soon—and nearly every day after that for a long time.

Cassius Clay later changed his name to Muhammad Ali. He became famous worldwide for his unmatched speed and skill in the boxing ring. Sports fans admired his courage. He was exciting to watch and they enjoyed his sense of humor.

But Ali's true greatness has shown itself outside the boxing ring. He has always stood up for his beliefs. When boxing made him famous, he used his fame to fight **racism** and poverty. Today he is known for his bravery, his generosity, and his strength.

Muhammad Ali may be most famous for winning the **heavyweight** *championship three times, something no boxer had ever done before.*

Muhammad Ali has always loved to spend time with his fans.

Cassius Clay was close to his parents and his brother.

Chapter Two

THE EARLY ROUNDS

assius Clay was born in Louisville, Kentucky, on January 17, 1942. His mother, Odessa, was quiet and religious. She was her son's role model. His father, Cassius Clay Sr., was fiery and artistic. He gave Cassius his courage and bold personality. Cassius also had a younger brother named Rudy.

The Clay family owned a home in a middle-class neighborhood. Still, black people and white people in Louisville lived in separate worlds. Like many southern cities at the time, Louisville had **segregation** laws. These laws kept black people and white people apart.

At that time, black people in many places in the United States couldn't eat in the same restaurants as white people. They couldn't sit with whites at theaters or ball games. Black children couldn't attend the same schools or share classrooms with white children.

Blacks faced other kinds of **discrimination**, too. They had a difficult time finding good jobs

Segregation was a large part of the society in Kentucky, where Cassius Clay grew up.

and many were stuck in jobs that didn't pay well. This treatment angered Cassius's father. He believed that he could have been a successful artist in an **integrated** world. Instead, he painted signs for a living.

• Cassius Jr. shared his father's frustration. At an early age, he dreamed of helping blacks live better lives. Cassius was also deeply moved by the 1955 murder of Emmett Till, a young black man who was brutally killed in Mississippi for talking to a white female shopkeeper. This event had a lasting effect on Cassius. He felt as if he had been born to do something meaningful for his people.

Boxing quickly became Cassius's passion. It was the most important thing in his life. He knew it would take work to become a champion. Day after day, month after month, he trained to get stronger. He practiced punching. He worked on his endurance.

Sometimes Cassius raced the bus in his neighborhood on his way to Central High, the racially segregated school he attended. This was part of his training.

Cassius Clay was never shy about getting attention for himself, especially before a big fight. He poses here in a photo taken in 1962.

The 1960 Olympics were held in Rome, Italy. Cassius Clay boxed in the light-heavyweight division.

Training wasn't easy, and he didn't always like it. Still, Cassius made himself work even when he didn't want to. Cassius was very disciplined in his training and was remarkably committed to improving his skill.

By the time he was 16 years old, Cassius weighed 170 pounds (77 kg) and was six feet (183 cm) tall. His boxing skill was also growing. In 1960, Cassius Clay turned 18 and won first place at the National Golden Gloves Championship, an important honor in amateur boxing. An amateur is a person who competes for pleasure, not for money. He also graduated from Central High School. His work was beginning to pay off. That summer, Cassius won a gold medal in the Olympics. It was a big accomplishment, especially for someone as young as he was. Cassius Clay was on his way to a **professional** boxing career.

Cassius Clay's fans greeted him when he returned home to Louisville, Kentucky, in 1964.

Chapter Three

THE GREATEST

assius Clay loved to talk about himself. He bragged that he was the smartest champ, the prettiest champ, the fastest champ, and, of course, the greatest champ. Sometimes he bragged about himself with poems. The poems attracted attention, and Clay loved attention—especially before a fight. He even used his poetry to predict the end of fights. "They all fall in the round I call," Clay declared.

Clay was a star in the ring. His movements were graceful and smooth. Boxing experts were amazed. They had never seen such a big man move so quickly. Experts also commented on his unique style. Even though he kept his hands low, Clay was quick enough to dodge punches and defend himself.

Many fights did end in the round that Clay predicted. He was correct in 13 of his first 17 fights as a professional boxer!

Over the next few years, Clay won his first 19 fights as a professional. When he was 22, he was scheduled to fight Sonny Liston, the reigning heavyweight boxing champion. Liston terrified opponents with his brutal power. He agreed to defend his title against Clay on February 25, 1964.

Sports fans weren't convinced that Clay could win. Liston wasn't worried. He was strong and overconfident. He thought Clay would be easy to beat.

Before the fight, Clay's assistant told him to "float like a butterfly and sting like a bee." When he got into the ring, Clay did just that. Liston wasn't able to hit Clay because he couldn't keep up with him. Cassius Clay was just too fast. While Clay danced around the ring, Liston stumbled.

By the sixth round, Clay was at his best. Liston looked tired and beaten. Liston quit and wouldn't come out for the seventh round. He said he had an injured shoulder. Cassius Clay went wild. He howled and jumped around the ring. "I shook up the world," he screamed. He had won the heavyweight title at only 22 years of age.

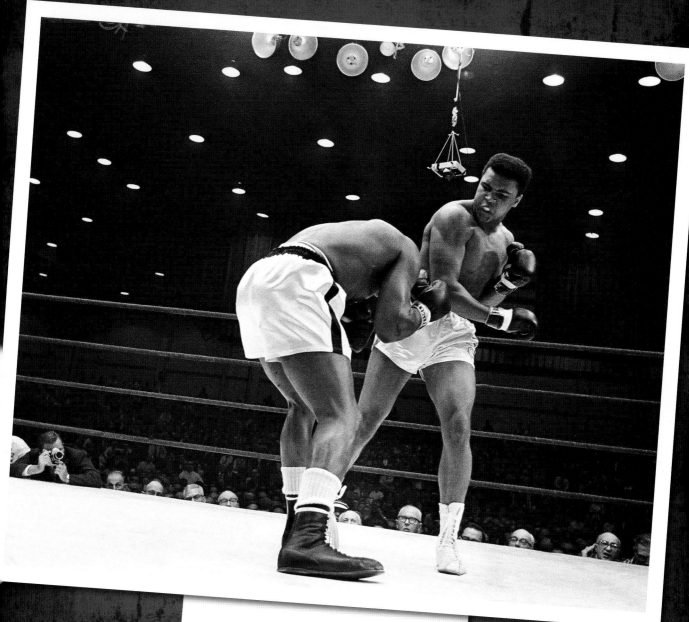

Cassius Clay won his first heavyweight title when he beat Sonny Liston in 1964.

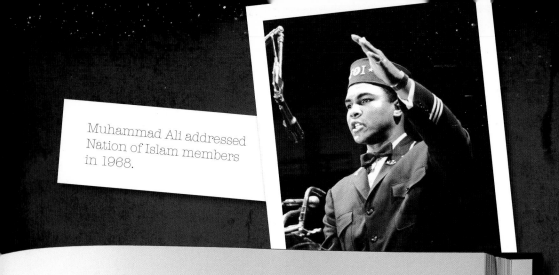

Chapter Four

THE TOUGHEST FIGHT

 assius Clay shocked the world when he took the heavyweight title away from Sonny Liston. After the fight, he shocked the world again. He told reporters that he was a member of a group called the **Nation of Islam**.

The Nation of Islam isn't actually part of the **Islamic religion**. The Nation of Islam was founded on the basis of peace. At the time, members of the Nation of Islam believed that blacks would be better off living in a separate society, away from whites. They felt it was the only way that black people would have equal rights.

Clay first heard about the Nation of Islam at a boxing tournament in 1959. Two years later, he attended a Nation of Islam meeting. Clay later said that joining the group changed his life.

Malcolm X was a leader of the Nation of Islam and an important spokesman for the group. Before the Liston fight, he often visited Clay. There were rumors that Clay had joined the group, but the public didn't know for certain until after the fight. Soon the Nation of Islam's leader, Elijah Muhammad, gave Cassius Clay a new name: Muhammad Ali.

Many Americans didn't like Ali's decision to join the Nation of Islam. But Ali had lived with the unfairness of segregation and was drawn to the Nation of Islam for its focus on self-respect and self-reliance. It angered him that the color of his skin limited his freedom. He had won an Olympic gold medal for the United States. He was the heavyweight champion of the world. Yet he still couldn't eat in some Louisville restaurants because he was black.

Ali had fought in the boxing ring and won. Now he wanted to focus on improving the lives of black people. He believed that joining the Nation of Islam was one way to do it.

White people and black people reacted negatively. Ex-heavyweight champion Floyd Patterson was especially angry. Patterson was black, too.

The name Muhammad *means "praiseworthy." The name* Ali *means "exalted" or "elevated."*

Muhammad Ali met Malcolm X (left), an influential leader in the Nation of Islam.

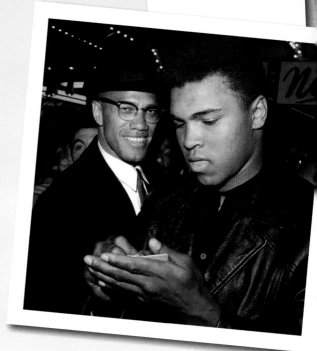

15

He looked down on Ali for joining the Nation of Islam because of its ideas about separating blacks from whites. Patterson believed that integration was a better path.

Ali's greatest fight was still to come, however, and it would take place outside the ring. The United States entered the Vietnam War in 1964. During the war, many young American men were **drafted** into the **armed forces**. The draft had been used in previous wars in U.S. history, such as World War II. When people are drafted, it is illegal for them to refuse to join the military unless they are unfit for service or **exempt**. Men drafted might be exempt on moral or medical grounds, for example. In 1967, Ali was drafted, but he refused to join the armed forces. He said he couldn't participate in a war because it was against his strong religious beliefs.

Ali appeared for his **induction** into the military on April 28, 1967. An officer called his name and told him to stand up. Ali refused. His name was called twice more. Ali refused twice more. The officer warned Ali that he was committing a crime. He told Ali that he could be punished. Ali still refused to step forward.

Finally, Ali was arrested. Some people suggested that Ali was simply trying to get out of serving in the army. They didn't believe that his religious beliefs were that strong. The boxing world also turned its back on him. His heavyweight title was taken away. Many states canceled his boxing license. Muhammad Ali, "The Greatest," was no longer allowed to box professionally in the United States.

Muhammad Ali also had his passport taken away and was unable to travel outside of the United States. This meant that he couldn't box anywhere in the world.

Muhammad Ali and his attorney, Edward Jocko (wearing hat), went to the Veterans building in Louisville, Kentucky, to appeal his draft classification.

In August of 1967, Ali married Belinda Boyd. Belinda shared Ali's religious beliefs. In their years together, they had four children.

Muhammad Ali received a great deal of media attention when he refused to enter the armed forces after being drafted.

Ali's trial took place in June of 1967, and the jury found him guilty. He decided to appeal the ruling. This meant that he attempted to change the decision by asking a higher court to consider the case.

Ali continued to attend Nation of Islam meetings. He studied the teachings of Elijah Muhammad. He traveled the country to meet with other Nation of Islam members. He spoke to people at Muslim **mosques** and on college campuses.

Ali couldn't box at professional boxing events for more than three years. But in 1970, Ali was able to get his license to box again. This meant that he could box professionally once more. Muhammad Ali returned to the ring on October 26, 1970. His opponent was Jerry Quarry. Ali won in just three rounds.

Ali won a much more important fight on June 28, 1971. The Supreme Court decided that Muhammad Ali wasn't guilty of avoiding the draft. Ali wouldn't have to go to jail, nor would he have to pay the $10,000 fine. Muhammad Ali was thrilled, but he celebrated quietly.

Chapter Five

THE COMEBACK

li was 29 years old and hadn't boxed in more than three years. Some people wondered if he was still the world's best boxer. Had sports fans already seen him at his best? Even Ali wondered if he was still "The Greatest."

During Ali's long break from boxing, a tournament was held to determine the new heavyweight champion. The winner was Joe Frazier.

Once Ali returned to the ring, he agreed to fight Frazier. Frazier was unbeaten, but so was Ali. Never before had an unbeaten heavyweight champion fought an unbeaten ex-champion. It was billed as "The Fight of the Century."

On March 8, 1971, approximately 25,000 fans crammed into New York City's Madison

Joe Frazier knocked down Muhammad Ali during the last round of their fight.

Square Garden to see the fight. About 300 million people watched the fight on television.

Ali and Frazier climbed into the ring. The air practically crackled with excitement. The very first seconds of the fight were thrilling. In the same instant, Frazier and Ali both landed punches. This would be one incredible match.

Ali won the first two rounds, but he wasn't as fast as he once was. Frazier got the better of Ali in the next few rounds. By the eighth round, it appeared as if Ali was giving up. But things changed in the ninth round. Ali buried Frazier in a stream of lightning-fast punches. For the first time, Frazier backed away. Ali was fighting for his pride.

In the eleventh round, Frazier nearly knocked out Ali. But somehow, Ali managed to stay on his feet. Frazier landed another hard punch. Ali fell into the ropes. The bell rang to end the round.

Just 20 seconds into the last round, Frazier threw what became the most famous punch in boxing history. It knocked Ali flat on his back. Frazier won the match,

but both boxers ended up going to the hospital.

Ali vowed he would fight for the title again. He won his next ten fights. Fans believed he was on his way back. But he lost to Ken Norton on March 31, 1973. Ali's jaw was broken in the fight, but he didn't give up. Later that year, he beat Norton in a rematch. In the meantime, Joe Frazier lost the heavyweight title to George Foreman.

Ali fought Frazier on January 28, 1974 and won. Next, it was time to fight George Foreman. The fight was set to take place in Zaire, Africa. People called it "The Rumble in the Jungle."

Ali and Foreman departed for Africa in September 1974. Ali was inspired to see the independent blacks in the African nation. But few sports fans believed Ali would win. Many people called Foreman the "unbeatable champion."

Once again, Ali surprised everyone. In the second round, Ali led Foreman to the edge of the ring. Then he spread his feet wide and leaned on the ropes. Foreman landed one powerful punch after another. Ali covered

After Muhammad Ali lost to Joe Frazier, he ended up in the hospital.

Muhammad Ali has always been very loyal to his fans. When Ali was in Zaire, he thrived on the attention, and the people of Zaire loved him. He joked with old men. He hugged children. He chatted with families. He even did magic tricks.

21

Ali had a name for the strategy he used against George Foreman in Zaire: Rope-a-Dope.

his head with his arms and took Foreman's punches. He hardly threw any punches back. What was Ali thinking?

Ali had a new plan. He wanted Foreman to get tired. Then, when Foreman ran out of energy, he would attack. Foreman kept flailing away, round after round. It was a hot, humid night. Foreman grew more and more tired.

Foreman hadn't trained for a long fight. He thought he would beat Ali in the early rounds. But Ali wouldn't fall. In the eighth round, Ali knocked Foreman down with a flurry of punches. Foreman couldn't get up in time.

It was ten years since Ali had beaten Sonny Liston. It was seven years after he had been stripped of his title. But Ali had regained the title of heavyweight champion.

Ali's next major fight took place in the city of Manila in the Philippines. On October 1, 1975, he faced Joe Frazier again. This time, people called the fight the "Thrilla in Manila."

Ali dominated the early rounds. Frazier controlled the middle rounds. With four rounds to go, Ali was in trouble. But he reached deep inside himself for courage and strength. He took over in the thirteenth round. By the fourteenth round, Frazier's eyes were nearly swollen shut. When the bell rang for the fifteenth round, Frazier's manager threw in the towel, signaling that Frazier had given up. It was one of the most brutal fights of Ali's career, but he came out the winner.

Muhammad Ali (right) deflects
one of George Foreman's punches
during their fight in Zaire in 1974.

After defeating Frazier, Ali won his next six fights and was feeling fearless. He scheduled a fight against a young boxer named Leon Spinks. Spinks had fought only seven times as a professional boxer. Ali thought he would be easy to beat. He didn't train as hard as he could have.

On February 15, 1978, Spinks surprised Ali and boxing fans. In the fifteenth round, Spinks defeated Ali and became the new heavyweight champion.

Ali made sure he was ready for his rematch against Spinks on September 15, 1978. He was in fantastic shape and won the fight. Ali became the first boxer to win the heavyweight title three times.

But Ali was ready to stop fighting. On June 27, 1979, he announced his plan to retire. However, a little more than one year later, he agreed to fight Larry Holmes for the title. Ali still loved attention, and the winner would get $8 million. Ali couldn't say no.

The fight took place in Las Vegas on October 2, 1980. For ten horrible rounds, Holmes pounded Ali. Several times, Holmes looked at the referee, hoping he would stop the fight. He finally did, and Ali spent the next two days in a hospital. Ali fought one more match against Trevor Berbick in 1981 and then retired for good.

Leon Spinks was young and inexperienced. He shocked everyone when he beat Ali.

Muhammad Ali participated in the opening ceremonies of the 1996 Summer Olympics in Atlanta, Georgia.

Chapter Six

THE MOST FAMOUS MAN IN THE WORLD

ears later, in 1996, the world watched the opening ceremonies of the Summer Olympics in Atlanta, Georgia. Boxer Evander Holyfield brought the Olympic torch into the stadium. He handed it off to swimmer Janet Evans. She circled the track.

Muhammad Ali stepped into the stadium and into the spotlight. He took the flame from Evans. With 300 million people watching, he lit the flame to signal the start of the Olympic Games. The emotion of the moment brought tears of joy to many.

But other people were saddened. The 54-year-old Ali looked very different from the champion

Today, Muhammad Ali has a happy relationship with his fourth wife, Lonnie. They were married in 1986. The two of them have an adopted son. Muhammad Ali has nine children in all.

Muhammad Ali helped with the release of hostages in Iraq in 1990. Afterward, a hostage met with Ali to thank him.

people remembered. His arms trembled as he lit the flame. He didn't look like the self-confident boxer that he once was. What had happened to the mighty heavyweight champ?

The years following his retirement had been difficult for Ali. He missed boxing. He had money problems. But his biggest problem was poor health.

In 1982, doctors noted that Ali had many symptoms like those of **Parkinson's disease**. He was later diagnosed with the disease. People with Parkinson's shake or tremble, have poor balance, and have trouble speaking. Although Ali experiences all of these difficulties, his mind is still sharp. The illness isn't life-threatening. His friends say Ali has developed a new sense of peace. He still has his deep religious beliefs. Today, he practices a different form of Islam, one that is committed to racial equality and integration.

Muhammad Ali has spent much of his time raising money to help people in need. He has raised money to pay for research to fight Parkinson's disease. He continues to raise money to feed

the hungry around the world. He has also spoken out against youth violence and racism to audiences around the country.

Ali helps people all over the world. He has traveled to Africa, Asia, and Latin America to bring food and money to the poor. In 1990, he went to Iraq during the Gulf War. His visit with Iraqi leader Saddam Hussein helped bring about the release of U.S. hostages.

Muhammad Ali has given sports fans a wealth of memories. At 18, he won an Olympic gold medal. By the time he was 22, he was the heavyweight champion of the world. In 1978, he became the first boxer to win the heavyweight title three times.

Muhammad Ali did all these things and more. His skill, speed, and bravery made him the greatest boxer of all time. His compassion and faith have made him "The Greatest" outside the boxing ring too. He works hard. And he never gives up, no matter how hard the fight.

Muhammad Ali still attends many public events with his wife, Lonnie.

TIME LINE

1940 **1950** **1960**

1942
Cassius Clay is born in Louisville, Kentucky, on January 17.

1954
Clay learns to box at the Columbia Gym in Louisville.

1959
Clay learns about the Nation of Islam.

1960
Clay graduates from Central High School in Louisville. He wins an Olympic gold medal and his first professional fight.

1964
Clay wins the heavyweight title. After the fight, he announces that he is a member of the Nation of Islam. He changes his name to Muhammad Ali.

1965
Ali successfully defends his heavyweight title against Sonny Liston with a knockout in the first round.

1967
Ali refuses to join the armed forces because of his religious beliefs. A jury convicts him of avoiding the draft. Ali appeals the verdict. He loses his championship title and can't box in the United States.

1970
Ali returns to the boxing ring. He beats Jerry Quarry and Oscar Bonavena in his first two fights in more than three years.

1971
The Supreme Court reverses Ali's conviction. Ali loses to Joe Frazier in a heavyweight championship fight. The battle is called "The Fight of the Century."

1974
Muhammad Ali beats Joe Frazier and George Foreman. He is the heavyweight champion of the world for the second time.

1978
Ali loses the heavyweight title to Leon Spinks on February 15. He wins it back on September 15 and becomes the first three-time heavyweight champ.

1979
Ali announces his retirement.

1980
Ali returns to the ring for a fight against Larry Holmes. Referees stop the fight after ten rounds, and Holmes is the winner. Ali spends two days in the hospital.

1981
Ali fights the last match of his career. He retires from boxing for good.

1984
Ali learns that he has Parkinson's disease.

1990
Ali is elected to the Boxing Hall of Fame.

1990
Ali travels to Iraq to promote peace. Iraqi leader Saddam Hussein releases hostages after Ali's visit.

1996
Ali lights the torch at the opening ceremonies of the Summer Olympics in Atlanta, Georgia.

GLOSSARY

armed forces
(*armd for-sez*)
The armed forces are groups of soldiers that protect a nation. Ali refused to join the U.S. armed forces and go to war because of his religious beliefs.

discrimination
(*diss-krim-i-nay-shun*)
Discrimination is unfair treatment of people based on differences of race, gender, religion, or culture. Ali suffered discrimination because he was black.

drafted
(*draf-ted*)
If a young man is drafted, he has been selected to join the armed services. Ali was drafted in 1967.

exempt
(*eg-zempt*)
To be exempt means you do not have to participate in something. Ali claimed he was exempt from the draft for religious reasons.

heavyweight
(*hev-ee-wayt*)
A heavyweight is a boxer who weighs more than 200 pounds (90 kg). Ali fought as a heavyweight.

induction
(*in-duk-shun*)
An induction is a meeting in which a person is admitted into an organization. Ali went to his induction into the armed forces, but refused to join the military.

integrated
(*in-tuh-gray-ted*)
When different things are combined together into one group, they are integrated. Cassius Clay Sr. believed his life would have been different if Louisville had been racially integrated.

Islamic religion
(*is-lahm-ik ri-lij-un*)
The Islamic religion is based on the teachings of a prophet named Muhammad. Ali is a follower of Islam.

mosques
(*mahsks*)
Mosques are Muslim places of worship, similar to churches. Ali visits mosques all over the world.

Nation of Islam
(*nay-shun of is-lahm*)
The Nation of Islam is a religious group that was founded on the principle of peace. Ali announced that he was a member of the Nation of Islam in 1964.

Parkinson's disease
(*par-kin-sunz duh-zeez*)
Parkinson's disease is an illness that causes tremors and muscle weakness. Ali suffers from Parkinson's disease.

professional
(*pruh-fesh-uh-nul*)
A professional is a person who is paid to do something. Ali was a professional boxer.

racism
(*ray-sih-zum*)
Racism is the belief that one race is superior to another. Racism was a part of the culture in Louisville, Kentucky, where Ali grew up.

segregation
(*seg-ruh-gay-shun*)
The act of keeping race, class, or ethnic groups apart is segregation. Ali grew up in a segregated society.

FURTHER INFORMATION

Books

Golus, Carrie. *Sports Heroes and Legends: Muhammad Ali*. New York: Barnes & Noble, 2006.

Grabowski, John F. *Boxing*. Farmington Hills, MI: Lucent Books, 2003.

Lewin, Ted. *At Gleason's Gym*. New York: Roaring Brook Press, 2007.

Smith, Charles R. *Twelve Rounds to Glory: The Story of Muhammad Ali*. Somerville, MA: Candlewick Press, 2007.

Ungs, Tim, and Daniel T. Kent. *Muhammad Ali and Laila Ali*. New York: Rosen Publishing Group, 2005.

Videos

A.K.A. Cassius Clay. Dir. Jim Jacobs. 1970. MGM, 2002.

Muhammad Ali: Made in Miami. PBS Home Video, 2008.

Web Sites

Visit our Web page for links about Muhammad Ali:

http://www.childsworld.com/links

NOTE TO PARENTS, TEACHERS, AND LIBRARIANS: We routinely verify our Web links to make sure they are safe, active sites—so encourage your readers to check them out!

Index